SCHOOL VIOLENCE

FEAR DOES NOT BELONG IN SCHOOLS

Kathleen A. Klatte

ROSEN
PUBLISHING

Published in 2024 by The Rosen Publishing Group, Inc.
2544 Clinton Street, Buffalo, NY 14224

First Edition

Editor: Greg Roza
Designer: Rachel Rising

Photo Credits: Cover, p. 1 Vineyard Perspective/Shutterstock.com; Cover, pp. 5, 3, 45 mimagephotography/ Shutterstock.com; Cover, pp. 1-48 Vitya_M/Shutterstock.com; Cover, Cosmic_Design/Shutterstock.com; pp. 3, 21 Daniel M Ernst/Shutterstock.com; pp. 3, 37 larry1235/Shutterstock.com; pp. 3, 40 Kate Way/Shutterstock.com; p. 6 kozhedub_nc/Shutterstock.com; pp. 7, 18 PeopleImages.com - Yuri A/Shutterstock.com; pp. 8, 9, 26 Rawpixel.com/ Shutterstock.com; p. 10 studiovin/Shutterstock.com; p. 11 SB Arts Media/Shutterstock.com; p. 13 Bogdan Sonjachnyj/ Shutterstock.com; p. 14 Tijana Simic/Shutterstock.com; pp. 15, 24 Monkey Business Images/Shutterstock.com; p. 16 VH-studio/Shutterstock.com; pp. 17, 35 LightField Studios/Shutterstock.com; p. 19 fotoNino/Shutterstock.com; p. 23 Gorodenkoff/Shutterstock.com; p. 25 F. JIMENEZ MECA/Shutterstock.com; p. 27 Dana Smith/Shutterstock.com; p. 27 https://commons.wikimedia.org/wiki/File:Tookie.jpg; p. 28 Daisy Daisy/Shutterstock.com; p. 29 Pixel-Shot/ Shutterstock.com; p. 31 Antonio Guillem/Shutterstock.com; p. 32 Prostock-studio/Shutterstock.com; p. 33 yurakrasil/ Shutterstock.com; p. 37 Eugene Powers/Shutterstock.com; p. 39 Vic Hinterlang/Shutterstock.com; p. 43 sirtravelalot/ Shutterstock.com.

Some of the images in this book illustrate individuals who are models. The depictions do not imply actual situations or events.

Library of Congress Cataloging-in-Publication Data

Names: Klatte, Kathleen A., author.
Title: School violence / Kathleen A. Klatte.
Description: Buffalo : Rosen Publishing, [2024] | Series: @rosenteentalk |
    Includes index.
Identifiers: LCCN 2023005034 (print) | LCCN 2023005035 (ebook) | ISBN
    9781499469349 (library binding) | ISBN 9781499469332 (paperback) | ISBN
    9781499469356 (ebook)
Subjects: LCSH: School violence--United States--Juvenile literature. |
    School violence--Psychological aspects. | School violence--Social
    aspects.
Classification: LCC LB3013.3 .K52 2024 (print) | LCC LB3013.3 (ebook) |
    DDC 371.7/8--dc23/eng/20230210
LC record available at https://lccn.loc.gov/2023005034
LC ebook record available at https://lccn.loc.gov/2023005035

Manufactured in the United States of America

CPSIA Compliance Information: Batch #CSRYA24. For Further Information contact Rosen Publishing at 1-800-237-9932.

Find us on

CONTENTS

Chapter 1

A Safe Place?

All through the COVID-19 **quarantine**, I kept hearing how important it was to get the schools back open. But if it's so important, why isn't it safe? I just learned that last year, in 2022, there were 51 school shootings. I think I would feel less worried if I was going to school at home on my computer again.

I read about a Swedish girl named Greta Thunberg who speaks out for action to address **climate change**. She staged "Fridays for Future" school strikes to push governments to take action. Lots of important people listen to her.

Today we're going to try that here. Kids at lots of schools are planning to walk out of class to protest the laws that make it so easy for bad people to get guns. I'm going to do that too. I don't care if I get in trouble. This is important to me.

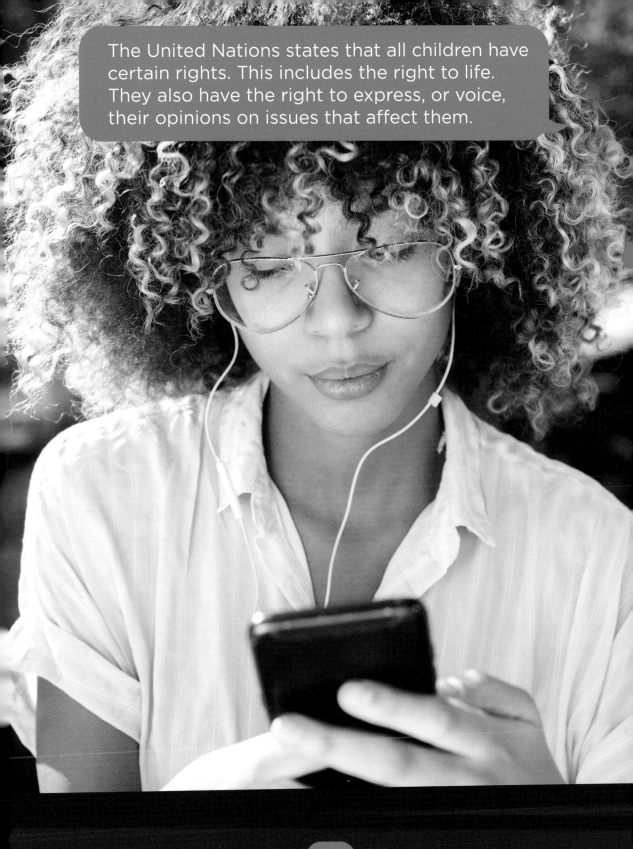

The United Nations states that all children have certain rights. This includes the right to life. They also have the right to express, or voice, their opinions on issues that affect them.

A SERIOUS PUBLIC HEALTH PROBLEM

Schools should be safe, orderly places for kids to learn. This includes traveling to and from school and going to school events. Sadly, that's not always the case.

The Centers for **Disease** Control and Prevention (CDC) defines school violence as "violence that occurs in a school setting." School violence is considered a public health problem. It's hard for kids to learn if they're worried. Teachers and staff should pay attention to teaching, not security and safety.

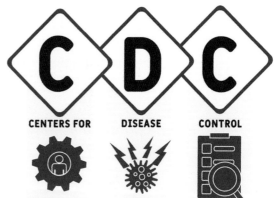

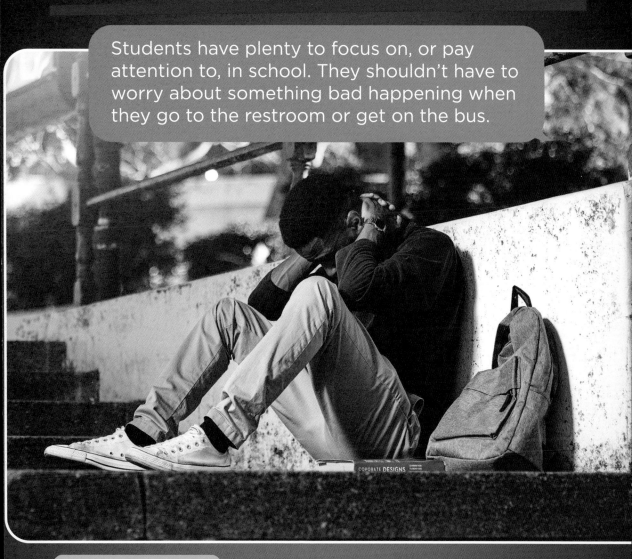

Students have plenty to focus on, or pay attention to, in school. They shouldn't have to worry about something bad happening when they go to the restroom or get on the bus.

CDC

The CDC is part of the U.S. government. It is a science-based group that aims to protect the health of all Americans. This group promotes healthy behaviors, or actions, and is watchful for new health threats, or dangers, such as the COVID-19 pandemic. You can read more about what the CDC does on its website: www.cdc.gov.

WHAT'S IN THE NEWS?

Columbine. Sandy Hook. Robb Elementary. Most people have heard of the terrible **tragedies** that occurred in these schools. But what could have been done to stop them? And what's being done to prevent the next mass shooting?

Most mass shootings include a gun found in the shooter's home. Many mass shooters show signs of being troubled.

What do you think your school should do to prevent school shootings? Do you think there's a way to help someone before they become violent?

Communities with a gang presence may have gangs inside schools. However, gangs were not blamed in any of the deadliest school shootings. Those were carried out by one or two gunmen.

SEEKING HELP

Sandy Hook Promise is an organization founded by families who lost loved ones in the December 2012 shooting in Newtown, Connecticut. Their goal is to educate people to see the signs that can lead to violence in schools. Find out more at sandyhookpromise.org.

WHAT'S NOT IN THE NEWS?

Other forms of school violence don't attract as much attention. Bullying and fighting have been problems in schools for a long time. Some people say they're just part of growing up. Still, it's hard to **concentrate** on learning if you're afraid of someone hurting you. It's not nice to have people make fun of your name or clothes, either. Kids who identify as **LGBTQ** often face bullying and report feeling like school isn't a safe place to learn.

Vandalism is another form of violence. Who wants to spend time in a building where things are broken or covered with graffiti or paint?

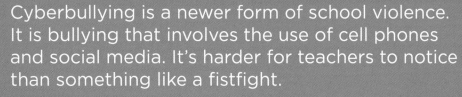

Cyberbullying is a newer form of school violence. It is bullying that involves the use of cell phones and social media. It's harder for teachers to notice than something like a fistfight.

DEFINING SCHOOL VIOLENCE

As we have seen, "violence in a school setting" can mean a lot more than school shootings. Bullying, vandalism, and fighting are all examples of violence. They can all result in a school setting that makes people feel unsafe. Coping, or dealing, with school violence has become an unfortunate reality of life, but it's one we don't have to settle for. Read on to learn more.

Chapter 2

A Closer Look

The posters went up for the senior prom today. Everyone's excited for one last big party before we graduate. My boyfriend and I thought it would be a blast to have a "fancy" date because we're going to different colleges next fall. But I'm really worried people will get mad because we are both boys.

Last year, two girls decided to go together. Some students didn't like it and said some nasty things to them before the event. One of the girls' cars was keyed in the student parking lot. Several parents also complained to the school board, saying the girls going together was against what their religion taught. What does that have to do with school anyway?

On the night of prom, one of the teachers hung out near the girls' table to make sure they were safe and had fun. I just wish it wasn't so hard on us kids.

Sometimes school violence begins at home. Just because your family holds harmful ideas doesn't mean you have to. LGBTQ kids are often the subjects of bullying. You can choose to be an ally, or friend.

WHY?

Poverty is a major factor in school violence. Poor areas where there is social injustice are more likely to have violence in schools. So are schools in places with high crime rates. **Substance abuse** and an unstable home life are factors that can affect affluent, or wealthy, kids as well as poor ones.

School violence affects teachers too. Many are afraid to break up fights among kids. Teachers have even reported being **threatened** or attacked by students.

School violence is a cycle, or repeating series of events, that feeds on itself. In order to break free, teachers, parents, community members, and students must work to address causes.

RISK FACTORS FOR SCHOOL VIOLENCE

- Violence in the home or neighborhood
- Unstable home life or low parental involvement
- Substance abuse by kids, parents, or peers
- Low grades or skipping school
- Friends or siblings who get into trouble

WHO'S AFFECTED?

School violence affects everyone in a community. Parents may worry about sending their kids to schools that aren't safe. Local business owners may worry about kids vandalizing or stealing from their shops. When a school gets a bad **reputation**, parents may pull their children from the school. The school might lose funding for special projects.

Kids who are afraid to go to school won't get good grades. Without good grades, they may not get good jobs. This is a cycle that needs to be broken.

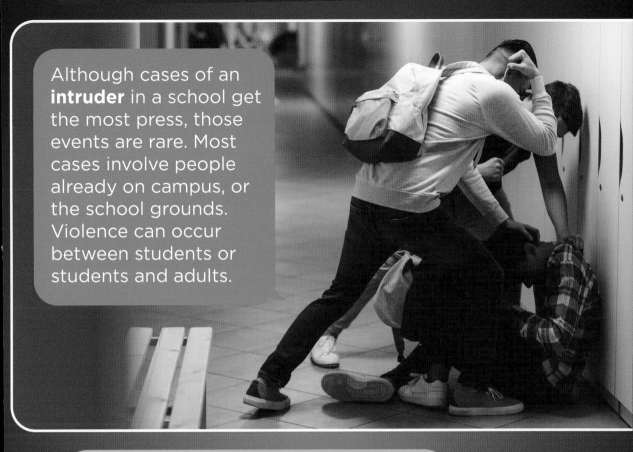

Although cases of an **intruder** in a school get the most press, those events are rare. Most cases involve people already on campus, or the school grounds. Violence can occur between students or students and adults.

ACCORDING TO A 2019 CDC SURVEY . . .

- About 20 percent of high school students reported being bullied.

- Eight percent of high school students reported being in a fight.

- More than seven percent reported being threatened or injured with a weapon.

- Almost nine percent stayed home from school at least one day because they didn't feel safe.

WHAT ARE THE CONSEQUENCES?

No one wants to spend time in a place where they don't feel safe. When kids are worried about getting hurt at school, they find reasons not to go. When you miss too much school, your grades suffer.

When teachers spend time breaking up fights, that's time taken away from teaching. When staff have to repair things that have been vandalized, that's time taken away from making the campus nicer. All these things add up to less learning for students.

Substance abuse can be both a cause and an effect of school violence. People might turn to alcohol to relieve their unhappiness about school. Drug dealers are often armed, adding more danger to the situation.

CONSEQUENCES

The consequences, or results, of school violence are wide-reaching.

- **Depression** and **anxiety** (students and staff)
- Reduced funding for education (either due to students being removed from the school or money being spent on additional security)
- Poor grades among students
- Higher risk of student death by suicide, or killing oneself

Chapter 3

Situations of Violence

I'm a junior in high school. My friends and I are researching colleges. It's exciting, but I just crossed one school off my list of places I want to apply to. I saw a story in the news about a girl who was **raped** at a party on the campus. She's only a few years older than me.

It's scary to think about something like that happening to me or my friends. I'm also really mad that the guy who did it didn't go to jail because he's the star pitcher on the baseball team. Why is his future more important than hers?

Students have the right to be safe at school. It doesn't matter if they're going to the library or going home from school.

HOW CLOSE IS TOO CLOSE?

Sexual violence is sexual activity that happens without your consent. Consent means someone freely and clearly agrees to participate in sexual activity with another. If you're younger than 18, you might not legally be able to agree to sexual activity.

You haven't consented to sexual activity if someone:

- Threatens to hurt you
- Says you have to have sex to be part of a group
- Offers you a better grade
- Offers to get you out of trouble
- Says you need to "prove you love them"

Get Help

The National Sexual **Assault** Hotline is available 24/7. It's free and confidential, or private. The number is 800-656-HOPE. Find out more at their website: www.rainn.org.

You never, ever "owe" anyone sex. Not the person you're dating. Not a school sports star. Not a teacher or other adult. No one.

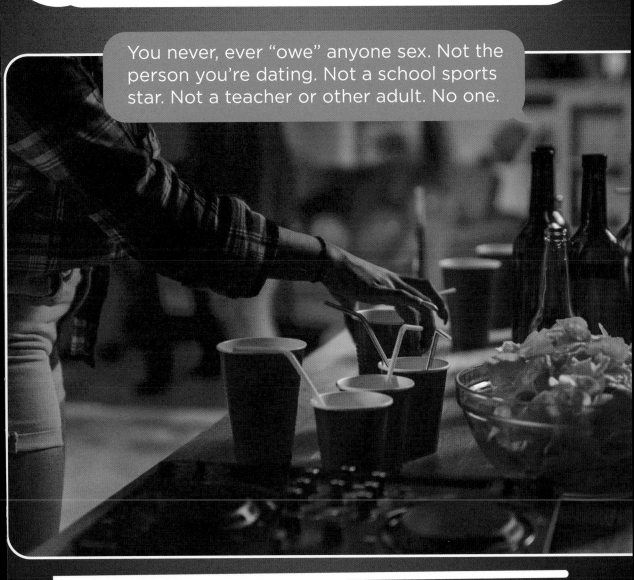

FIGHTING

You've likely seen kids push, shove, and hit to get their way since you were very young. It's never a good way to settle differences, or problems. When people fight, someone can be seriously injured, or hurt. There might be weapons involved, such as knives and guns. Depending on how serious a fight is, the consequences might be more than getting in trouble. It might even involve **criminal** charges. This can hurt your chances when applying for college or a job.

Even if someone else tries to start a fight, or says something really **offensive**, don't take the bait. Walk away. Tell a teacher or safety officer.

Martial arts training teaches self-defense skills. It also teaches mental discipline, or self-control. However, any effective martial arts school will teach students to avoid fights in the first place.

SELF-DEFENSE TRAINING

Training in the martial arts has many benefits. It's a great way to exercise and get in shape. Mastering skills and earning belts is beneficial for self-esteem. The discipline and hard work required to do well in any martial art are useful in other areas of life.

Tae Kwon Do is considered one of the best martial arts for teens. It's a full-body workout that develops strength and balance. Karate and jiu-jitsu are also good options. Regardless of the martial art one chooses, it's important to remember martial arts training should never be used to bully or hurt others.

GANGS

Gang activity in schools around the country is a serious problem. It's not just kids messing around. Gangs can be involved with weapons or drugs. They might even be involved in crimes involving sex. Depending on their age and the type of crime, they might be charged as adults in the criminal justice system. Becoming involved with a gang is something that can change your whole life for the worse.

> Have you ever seen gangs in your neighborhood or school? Have they affected your ability to go to school peacefully?

Get Help

The Safe School Helpline is a website created by students and educators. If you're older than 13, you can use it to anonymously, or secretly, report a violent event at your school. The form is available at safeschoolhelpline.com.

San Quentin State Prison

CHANGE OF HEART

Stanley "Tookie" Williams (1953–2005) was a convicted murderer. That means he was found guilty by a court of killing someone. As a teen, he helped found the Crips, a dangerous gang in Los Angeles. During many years in prison, he regretted, or felt bad, about his actions. He wrote books to convince kids not to join gangs. He was **nominated** for the Nobel Peace Prize five times. However, he was executed (put to death) for his crimes in 2005.

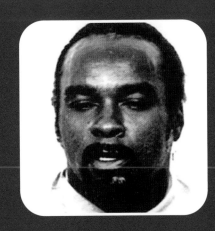

BULLYING

Pointing and laughing at the new kid with thick glasses. Making fun of the way someone talks or the color of their skin. Knocking things out of a smaller kid's hands. Mocking someone's **gender expression**. These are all examples of bullying.

It's important to break the cycle of bullying. Some bullies are abused, or treated in harmful and harsh ways, at home. Some kids who've been bullied even take their own lives.

Even if it hasn't happened to you, you've seen it or heard about it. Bullying isn't good for anyone. Kids who have been bullied have been known to hurt themselves or others. Kids who are bullies often have problems of their own.

If you see someone being bullied, speak up. Tell the bully to stop. Get a teacher or safety officer. Make sure a trusted adult knows what's going on.

Get Help

Teens Against Bullying is a website created by teens. It's full of age-appropriate resources for dealing with bullying. Find out more at TeensAgainstBullying.org.

It's not enough to just stop someone from being bullied. Include them at lunch or in an activity. Let them know they're not alone.

CYBERBULLYING

Cyberbullying involves electronic devices (such as smartphones and tablets) and social media. Cyberbullying might include:

- Texting someone mean messages
- Tagging someone in a fun activity they were left out of
- Responding to someone's social media post or video with a mean comment or post
- Mean comments while playing video games

Be careful who you give your cell phone number to. Ask your folks to help you set your social media accounts to "friends only" or private. Be careful who you connect with online and block them if they do anything that makes you uncomfortable.

Get Help

StopBullying.gov is a website of resources for kids and adults. It has information on bullying and cyberbullying. It's a U.S. government website and includes information, or facts, on federal laws concerned with **discrimination**.

Many social media sites have ways to flag inappropriate or offensive messages or posts. If you're in an online chat room, you may be able to report the offensive behavior to a moderator, or the person in charge of making sure everyone follows the rules of the chat room.

WORDS MATTER

Making fun of other people is never OK. Some forms of **harassment** go beyond just being annoying or upsetting. Bullying that's based on a person's race, **ethnicity**, or gender expression is a **violation** of federal civil rights laws. Discrimination that leads to violence may be considered a hate crime.

Some people may choose to dress a certain way. It might be because of their religion or culture. It might just be what they're comfortable wearing. It's fine to ask them questions about what they're wearing to learn more about them. It's never OK to make fun of them.

Schools are required to stop this behavior. If they don't, you can file a complaint with the U.S. Department of Education's Office for Civil Rights. You can find out more online at ed.gov.

A person expressing their personality through their choice of clothing is just as worthy of respect as someone wearing religious clothing.

TITLE IX

Title IX is a federal law that was passed in 1972. It requires all schools that receive federal funding to provide sports teams for both boys and girls. However, the law also applies to all other aspects of campus life. It also ensures gender equality in all schools that receive federal funding.

ASAD'S STORY

I hate gym class. Who cares about running around chasing balls? It's stupid. I'm no good at it, but the teacher makes me play anyway. Then the jocks always bother me in the locker room because I messed up their game. Last week they threw my books in the shower and walked away laughing.

I told the teacher that I'm not happy in gym class, but he doesn't care. I'm going to say I'm sick next time. Then maybe they'll leave me alone. Or maybe I'll just skip school. I like school most of the time, but I can't take the bullying anymore.

Not everyone is good at team sports or games. It doesn't mean you're not physically fit. Lots of people have fun with different types of activities.

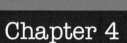

Chapter 4

SCHOOL SHOOTINGS IN THE UNITED STATES

School shootings are rare, compared to fighting or bullying. However, they're so horrible that they attract lots of media attention. For example, many parents in New York know details, or facts, about the 2022 school shooting at Robb Elementary in Uvalde, Texas.

Most school shooters use guns found in their home. This sparks arguments about stricter gun control laws. While this can cause inaction, in 2022, U.S. president Joe Biden signed a set of major gun safety policies into law.

Get Help

March for Our Lives is a student led organization. They rally for better gun control laws. Find out more at marchforourlives.com.

The Second Amendment to the United States Constitution talks about the right to "keep and bear arms." Many people think this ensures their right to own guns. Others think guns are too easy to get. What do you think?

YOUNG ACTIVIST

Naomi Wadler is a gun reform activist from Alexandria, Virginia. An activist is someone who supports action to create change. At age 11, Wadler organized a school walk-out to protest the shooting at Marjory Stoneman Douglas High School in Parkland Florida. She was the second-youngest speaker at the 2018 March for Our Lives rally.

COMMUNITY REACTIONS

Communities try to keep schools safe. Since the Columbine High School shooting in 1999, active-shooter drills have become all too common. Some schools require guests to be buzzed in through locked doors. Others have **metal detectors** or police on campus.

Some schools are being redesigned. They'll offer better places for students to shelter or break up lines of sight for a gunman. Following the shooting at Robb Elementary School in Uvalde, Texas, some Texas schools issued DNA kits to help parents identify, or name, their children in case of an emergency. DNA is a substance that carries genetic information, or information passed on from parents, in animal and plant cells.

There have been suggestions to arm teachers. Many teachers don't like the idea of having guns in the classroom. They don't think they should be expected to confront a gunman.

WHAT'S THE ANSWER?

Many people think more security is the answer to school shootings. Some people have suggested training teachers to use and carry guns in school. Others think improved background checks and mental health checks should be necessary when buying a gun. Do you think these are effective ways to stop school shootings from happening?

Chapter 5

BREAKING THE CYCLE

Some argue that many communities' reactions to school violence don't do enough to prevent these tragic events. Increasing security just assumes that school will always be a dangerous place. It can be scary to think about facing **lockdowns** and wearing bulletproof backpacks to school.

Many schools have hired security officers and use metal detectors to watch out for guns and other weapons. However, school violence remains a problem for many communities in the United States.

So what can your school do differently? What can YOU do differently? It may sound weird to you, but you can start by being an ally to other students in need of help. Often kids who become violent feel left out or bullied.

Making a Difference

The American Civil Liberties Union (ACLU) has programs to help young people become more active in issues that affect their communities. It holds a National Advocacy Institute each summer in Washington D.C. Other youth programs may be available in your state. You can learn more abou the ACLU at their website: www.aclu.org.

WHERE TO GET HELP

Most schools have counselors, or workers who can help students with social and emotional needs. Many teachers are caring people who want their students to be safe and do well. Some schools may also offer a confidential tip hotline. Here are a few more resources for people in need of help.

- Substance Abuse and Mental Health Services Administration's (SAMHSA's) Disaster Distress Hotline: 1-800-985-5990

- National Suicide & Crisis Lifeline: text or call 988

- Gay, Lesbian, Bisexual and Transgender National Hotline: 1-888-843-4564

BE AN ALLY

Being an ally means standing up for people who are being bullied or facing discrimination. Being an ally can mean telling someone to stop making offensive comments. It doesn't mean you put yourself in harm's way. If someone is being threatened, go get a teacher, counselor, or safety officer.

WAYS TO BE AN ALLY

- Listen when people speak. Don't talk over them—they know their own experience better than you.

- Be open-minded. Things you've heard all your life aren't always correct.

- If someone tells you your words are offensive—even if you didn't mean it—say you're sorry.

- Include kids of different races and backgrounds in your circle.

- If someone makes an offensive joke or uses mean words, correct them politely—yes, even adults.

Being an ally can mean asking your friend to educate you about how their background is different from yours. All of us have ideas we've grown up with. Sometimes we can be **racist** or **phobic** without realizing it. Learning about others who may be different from you helps you become a more open-minded and caring person.

When someone tells you that something is racist or offensive, listen to them. Sometimes things you've heard all your life are just plain wrong. If they tell you they prefer certain pronouns, use them. Listen, learn, and be better.

A Matter of Pride

Desmond Napoles is a teen drag performer, fashion artist, and LGBTQ+ rights activist. They are also the author of *Be Amazing: A History of Pride*. Napoles and their family were subjected to investigations, prompted by complaints from members of the community who disapproved of their outgoing personality and activism. In time, the cases were ended and called "unfounded." Napoles continues to stand up for LGBTQ+ communities, and they are known to tell people "Be yourself, always."

STANDING UP

I was pretty nervous, but I did it. At noon, I closed my book and stood up. So did a bunch of other kids. The teacher said if we left, she'd have to mark us absent. I told her I understood, but that this was important to us. She said she agreed, and that she was proud of us.

A bunch of parents and reporters were waiting outside. The principal came out and asked why we weren't in class. One of the seniors stepped up and said that we were protesting the laws that let people buy guns so easily. They read a list of people running for office who support better gun laws. Then the senior said they hoped our folks would vote for the people on the list, to keep us safe. My folks cheered for us. I might not be able to vote for a few years, but I'm glad I made my voice heard today.

You spend much of your time at school. You have the right to be safe while you learn.

GLOSSARY

anxiety: Fear or nervousness about what might happen.

assault: A violent or sudden attack.

climate change: Significant and long-lasting change in the Earth's climate and weather patterns; especially in current use, it is associated with global warming caused by human activities including burning fossil fuels.

concentrate: To give your attention to the thing you are doing, reading, etc.

criminal: Relating to a crime.

depression: A state of feeling sad. Also a mood disorder that involves lasting feelings of sadness and a loss of interest in activities.

discrimination: The practice of unfairly treating a person or group of people differently from other people or groups of people.

disease: An illness.

ethnicity: Of or relating to races or large groups of people who have the same customs, religion, origin, etc.

gender expression: The physical and behavioral manifestations of one's gender identity.

harassment: The act of creating a hostile or unpleasant situation for someone through unwanted contact.

intruder: A person who enters a place illegally.

LGBTQ: Acronym for lesbian, gay, bisexual, transgender and queer or questioning.

lockdown: An emergency measure or condition in which people are temporarily prevented from entering or leaving a restricted area or building (such as a school) during a threat of danger.

martial arts: A type of self-defense or fighting that's practiced as a sport.

metal detector: A security tool that finds hidden metal objects, particularly guns and knives.

nominate: To put forward someone who deserves an honor, usually in a group of other people put forward for the same thing.

offensive: Causing someone to feel hurt, angry, or upset. Also something that is rude or insulting.

phobic: Having an intense hatred or dislike of something.

poverty: The state of being poor.

quarantine: The situation of being kept away from others to prevent a disease from spreading.

racist: The belief that some races of people are better than others.

rape: The crime of forcing someone to have sex by using violence or the threat of violence.

reputation: The common opinion that people have about someone or something.

substance abuse: Excessive use of alcohol or drugs.

threaten: To state an intention of hurting another person.

tragedy: A very bad event that causes great sadness and often involves someone's death.

vandalism: Willfully damaging property.

violation: The act of breaking a law or rule.

INDEX